The Wild Fox of Yemen

Winner of the Walt Whitman Award
of the Academy of American Poets
2020
Selected by Harryette Mullen

Sponsored by the Academy of American Poets,
the Walt Whitman Award is given annually to the winner
of an open competition among American poets
who have not yet published a book of poems.

The Wild Fox of Yemen

Poems

Threa Almontaser

Graywolf Press

This publication is made possible, in part, by the voters of Minnesota through a Minnesota State Arts Board Operating Support grant, thanks to a legislative appropriation from the arts and cultural heritage fund. Significant support has also been provided by Target Foundation, the McKnight Foundation, the Lannan Foundation, the Amazon Literary Partnership, and other generous contributions from foundations, corporations, and individuals. To these organizations and individuals we offer our heartfelt thanks.

MINNESOTA
STATE ARTS BOARD

CLEAN
WATER
LAND &
LEGACY
AMENDMENT

Published by Graywolf Press
250 Third Avenue North, Suite 600
Minneapolis, Minnesota 55401

All rights reserved.

www.graywolfpress.org

Published in the United States of America

ISBN 978-1-64445-050-5

2 4 6 8 9 7 5 3 1
First Graywolf Printing, 2021

Library of Congress Control Number: 2020938638

Cover design: Kimberly Glyder

CONTENTS

٣

In the caverns of its death
my country neither dies nor recovers. It digs
in the muted graves looking for its pure origins

—ABDULLAH AL-BARADOUNI

بلادي في كهوف الموت
لا تفى ولا تشفى
تنقّر في القبور الحرس
عن ميلادها الأصفى

عبدالله البردوني —

The Wild Fox of Yemen

١

Hunting Girliness

My girliness is the size of a Cerberus.
        I unchain it out my body, serpent tail tombing

                        a Mercedes, someone's Scissorhands
                        shrubs, trio-headed howls loudening

the clean suburb. It is not tasteful
        to fuck with the Tooth Fairy, baby teeth planted

                        in the oleanders. To beat up boys
                        at the park, make one my wife

in a white dress when we play marriage.
        My aunties crammed me with a mute troubadour

                        & a lame-folded fawn since birth. I am
                        a pressed-palmed girl promised palaces,

fountain of honey, flood of milk.
        Tell me why there is something else

                        powering inside, trying to get out,
                        pummeling my skin purple. Tell me,

when can I stop barbing my headscarves,
        lining my lashes with spears? I learn to love

                        my body by playing dead: legs man-
                        spreading, droop-lipped for vultures

to dine on my basking belly, wattle
        of female hanging from their beaks

                        & it's the only time I lie still.
                        My girliness is a whistle uphill,

& my mother is too far down to hear it.
        She says, *Stop being reckless*. I say, Truth is,

                I quit being cautious in third grade
                when the towers fell &, later, wore

the city's hatred as hijab. I believe my baby
        breasts are reckless, so I tape them down.

                Loop training bras to ceiling fans.
                Stay hairy. She pulls out her prayer mat,

enlists God to drag a sharp nail across
        my jaw as I sleep, shaving my girl beard off.

                So I carry copperheads into the kitchen
                as compensation, tails whipping raw

slaps on my chest. Their fangs bite air
        & I bite back until I creak when I talk.

                She beheads them with a meat knife
                then beats me blue, & I take everything

giggling. We all choose how to fill
        the lingering lack inside us: I lace bitch-loud

                boots to the knees. Scab soft skin
                on asphalt. Peel the grit whenever

my blood hardens. I am at war. I go out
        to hunt girliness. Find her crouched, camouflaged

                like a fugitive between the forsythias.
                I load my brother's BB gun, ignore

her old insistence, begging herself pink.
    There was never a day I claimed those flowers

                        or any hound that heeled.

Stained Skin

My aunties were birthed from the bottom of their mother's
tea cup, emerging out the fortunes and sugared milk.

They are still cinnamon. They trail black tea leaves
like loose hairs. Their skin simmering darker, darker,

and it is beautiful. I am twelve, pouring shai Arabi
in a crowded kitchen, showcasing henna I did

on my left hand—yam-colored stems, whirls
and Dragon Balls. Henna plants crushed to steep

in tea. My eczema prickles, ukhti wiping the tears.
I learn to find beauty in decay, paint my rash

as poplar leaves in fall, turning rutilant. I want kids
at school to see me tatted. I draw gang signs on arms

at lunch. Always seen me as something other.
Now I will be a cooler, exotic other. I want to be

rimmed kohl-black, look like my wide-hip aunts,
waist-length hair sprayed with shai. Husbands rivered

by a heavy curtain, pulling sweet blue from a coiled
pipe, our whole house a foggy smoke screen the ghosts

can hide in. I flaunt the henna hand to my ancestors,
their awe a *whoosh* of wind on our faces. I slip it

through the drape so the men can peek, rush off
like I just placed it in the jaws of a karkadann.

My aunties can leap their henna off their wrists.
The flowers dance on tabletops, fragrant us

into a brief history. Their patterns too detailed
to boggle. The careful speed in which they draw

on themselves. How they squeeze just the right
sum from cones: gooped paste, needle tip,

spool of zigzags in ten minutes. Jide cakes
only her soles. Fat circles in the middle of her palms.

Leaves the bodygarden for us younger girls, her skin
not what it once was. I know she sees me showing off,

rubbed raw with banana peels, olive oil, things
off YouTube, trying to smooth herself back.

None of us can escape the pure henna shipped
in suitcases of honeycombs, unseen relatives,

sunbaked stones. My aunties are spread eagle
on the couch, still as gargoyles in a graveyard,

unable to eat, dress, wipe their ass. I can't imagine
a day with their patience, turning lanky limbs

into a mysterious mural. I don't even see them
breathe, sleeping beauties, their little deaths, a cousin

paid to fan their odic skin until the stain dries,
cracks, the first crumble, a fresco flowering beneath.

Muslim Girl with White Guys, Ending at the Edge of a Ridge

If you shoot me, you better shoot straight. There is nothing like a wounded animal.

—MAXINE WATERS

١

I toss in Arabic when I can't find

a certain feeling, use my body—dipped chin,
head bob, eyebrow dance—when English

carousels completely. Neither muscle nor mouth
devoted to one way of speaking. Every language

I borrow from somewhere else. The guys notice,
compliment my accent. I have to catch myself

from telling them the same.

٢

White guys make me write their names in Arabic
to show their tattoo artist later. I am still recovering

from three days of Eid, full of farah wa figs,
in the habit of calling strangers *brother, sister.*

One rips the pin
off my headscarf, cuffs my wrist

with a big
hand, barbecue-
sticky. Presses
the needle's
tip

to my blue line, orb
of blood. Says,
*It feels like this
only deeper.*

۳

A new wreck ascends among the crowd: just last week, holy-month fasting
and force-fed cold fries, the body's song
a snake, jaw locked in place. *Open up.*
Just one piece. God
will forgive you.
Was what we dubbed as translation
really a squandered tongue rewinding?
Never will they interpret me correctly—
catalogue of lazy scribbles, sepia ink
spilling. I am set writhing on the table.

It is the gong of the poet's helve I listen for,
sword inscribing the air. I am going through
a change with each entitled inflection, each
freckled arm reading my waist. I become

calcified, a wild text raging.
The noises my windpipe makes,
aching for carnal speech, the relief
of no words. My face fissures—

I am not the same woman that walked onto campus. I am wind
rattling a creature's teeth,
the twitching comma stuck
in a throat, my blood ripening
into beast brine. They don't notice
my transformation, the seconds it took.
Once, I was a scripture, declarations so thunderous, so heard.

Recognized Language

Where did my old words go, my first words? I found my native speech like a trap
    door, the Arabic softening my fall. Now the words shed
    from my mouth like deciduous teeth. Sometimes I dream
    in Arabic without understanding. I search everyone's pockets,
    leave them hanging like panting tongues. I have been so careless
    with the words I already have. I don't remember how to say
    grape or niece or bright. I try calling Arabic back like wild horses.
    If I find them roaming a jilted road, sitting on an ancient turtle's
    back, dancing naked in the desert, I swear I'll fishnet pronouns
    so fast, swallow adjectives whole, knock verbs back with a burp.
    Tonight, I will light a nar to eat the dark, make myself inviting,
tendrils of lost words floating back to me, getting cozy again on the cushion of my tongue.

٢

As a baby, I crawled to the aja'iz,
their hands dripping blood.

               One took the head of a slaughtered goat

and made it talk so I would laugh.
I lifted ivory limbs from a pile

               not knowing in my small hands I held

the bones of the one that went *baa baa*
every morning, not knowing I held bones

               at all as I tapped them against each other,

smiled at the clicks they made,
somehow recognized the language.

3

deep themselves bury words missing My
soil American in
boil blood mother's my makes It
sound wrong the with wail I when
mouth my in
reflection my like off little a feel I
shrunk wa stretched door car a in
accent the want I back them want I
lugha songy-sing my back
Arabic in abki wa adhak to want I
bloodline my tasting hard down bite I
form I phrase every in

ع

Languages slip into our mouths like secondhand
smoke. But English grinds Arabic to white sand.

Now Baba keeps Arabic for scoldings, dirty
jokes, talking behind our backs. To calm his crying

sister on the phone, oceans away. He tells me,
Tudthkary! My shame. To live at the border—

tugging at Arabic's opulent web of words
without the whole sense of them. I only remember

some things: sunbathed maize burning my skin.
Dyed dresses sold for school pencils. A jide's

blind eyes glopping asal directly from the hive,
circle of bees around her head a buzzing halo,

without fear of the sting that comes with sweetness.

Etymology of Hair

The OG of hair was unbound & coil thick, without
violence. Back at the start, every head was a sun
entering into fistfuls of curls you could lose
a hand in, curls you could cry into.

Now, a girl's hair can shield her & turn her
into a wasp at once.

The etymology of *hair*
                    is *nest*, from the Arabic,

from my father's trimmer, glistening
& bulked like a filled beehive. I refused
to straighten. No mother on Steinway
knew what to do with hair fending for itself—

afraid to touch their daughters, the parts of them
left undomesticated.

& so I am sheared without
                    ceremony. *Hush, it's easier*

to manage this way. The strands fly over
skyscrapers, sticking to everyone like pollen.
Ode to my Gordian knots, twisted solid
with shea, stringing with beads & fish spines,

fence chains & forks. *I'm ugly*, God tells me, & I
believe him. I miss brown water

from hair playing in mud. I miss
                    our fights—one wild thing

encountering another, swaddled
in frizz, extension of my blood. &
the carpenters! When one got too close,
wings against scalp, the panicked tangle of us.

I pet the cactus. Wish my head were a blinding
white bulb, a giant

sunflower with extra sun.
                    I twist phantom braids in my sleep.

Shaytan Sneaks Bites of My Tuna Sandwich

Just walkin' the streets death can take you away
It's never guaranteed that you'll see the next day
At night the evil armies of Shaytan don't play
                                        —THE FUGEES

I believed in Shaytan before I believed in the Power Rangers: smoke-skinned, lore-loaded,
hooves for hands—

they will use my yawning mouth
as a toilet if I don't cover it. Sneak bites of my tuna sandwich if I forget to bless it first.

Before I believed in mighty morphin' protectors, I was told to vacuum every corner.
Gobble swarms of Shayateen from under sofas, coffee stands,

                                        but only dust bunnies and a paperclip puff out.

And yet.   I am still afraid to stay out after sundown. They might follow me home
as an animal—night-furred, to better focus their heat and devilish power. I am running

out of excuses to tell my friends when I leave in the middle of a movie. Box my dessert to go.
Shaytan can't steal me, can't take a nibble from my thigh

like the Tanglewood Kings. Everybody's second cousin is in the TK gang.
I look one in the eye outside his dad's gas station by the Dunkin' searching

for his inner dark. Who lifts a chin as if to say, *Mind your business.* Who just last week

pushed Nadia against the telephone pole, lifting her skinny fists like antennas to heaven,
old jam doughnuts bleeding the ground.
                                        Since then, she's stopped eating

and the world shifted four feet to the left, like the final bee had died and life
never moved the same.

If the devil had an address, it would be three stalls back   in a woman's highway restroom
where anything unspeakable can go down without a peep.

                              Be afraid the TV always tells me.

I saw a Shaytan at a red light in Apex, North Carolina.
His speckled hand reached over, drew a gun, pointed it
                              at my window, blowing
                              kisses, how he wanted to [   ]
                              in my [   ] until I [   ]
                              and begged for it.

I can't forget my mother's stories of the hidden always watching. Of all that can enter
a room and a body in silence. Can't forget her dry spit

                              when I wake from a nightmare. The three toofs

her mouth makes over my left shoulder, blistering the face
of Shaytan. The dates she pits and slips into my hand

each morning: wrinkled love notes, odd-numbered guardians, so sweet and so cold.

Muslim with Dog

I bring home a baby pit bull
in a Nike shoebox, her mother left tied to a post in the Bronx.
The puppy hops on hind legs, pees in a pot of yucca cane, licks the hollow
in my throat when she sleeps on my chest.

Muslims believe a dog's saliva is najasah.
They soap themselves seven times. They muzzle
their Minotaur dread, kennel it in a maze
wahda. The dread breaks loose, runs forward
as a dripping line of slobber slugged
at their bodies. A dog won't attack

the owner who abuses it. Once, a terrier was charged
with protecting a baby. The couple returned
to the canine out front, mouth full of blood,
and beat it dead. Inside was their child
beside a snake chewed to shreds.

There is a golden retriever being trained
to chase kids at the border. There is another
by a fireplace, head on someone's knee as they're stroked.
Both work hard for their purpose.
Neither wants to crouch alone in a parking lot
quivering against whatever wind

is rising. My grandfather can't recall
how one bared its fangs, ready to die for him
on McGowan St. at the hands of a white man megaphoning,
Leave your plague of filth back in the desert.
Nasi the time a starving collie carefully carried
its first kill, gave all it had, to his feet.

Consider the prostitute who passed a mutt
panting near a well. Who took off her shoe, tied it to her scarf,
drew up water for the dog, and God

forgave her. Him? He will hear the phone ring
and won't pick up. There is Yemen on the other end.
Six dogs and a village crier. Sunlight twizzling
the mountains. Divine messages in sand. The rabid dogs

are hungry, roaming for a man's remains, chunk
of a child's thigh as they play.
Savagery in Khormaksar looks like the same fur
that roams our block, in this borough that never rests, where we are
khayifeen, the city glinting blindly off our bodies.

Something on the street brushes my grandfather
like a wet nose, and he thinks the dogs
are back, occupying our hood, asking, *Where are your papers?*
In his dreams, the dogs tree him onto the roof of his store.
Each bark jitters the yellow lamp post, their eyes on him like a raid,
claws raking the glass. *No angels*

will enter our home, he tells my pit bull before tossing her into the big
bluestems, her whine a low nothing.
Long ago, in another land, he would hear a dog's growl and think,
comrade. To him, never was a noise less lonely—it sounded like his older brother
pouring al bahr over his head between waves.
But he won't let himself remember, shrouds it in the shade
of mosque domes. We learned helplessness

by shocking al kilab: bastards of brutes inside twisted
labyrinths, roving nowhere in a ringmaster's truncheon.
When the ashes of my animal get buried with me, how long until the ground erupts
with fountains of noor, a lambent nova
cresting high into the grandstand?

In the tall dusking blades I follow a refulgent string,
find her digging the soil alone, in search of something
to reclaim. My hands I plunge into her gold-happy fur,
my face in raqabatuha kulu, all of myself
where he is too afraid to reach.

Dream Interpretation [*Apricot*]

Slicing the rotten bits while a baboon pats henna in your hair means your family will be notified of your missing body.

One that grows a mouth and tries to kiss your cheeks four times means you will forget your mother's last name and then you won't remember she was ever your mother.

I am see-through, phantasmal, falling through floors from sighing. My mother tells the cops I have been MIA for days. They take lazy notes, can't recall our names. I sit right beside them. There is a baboon with talking hands. She signs the word for *cry*, trails a wrinkled finger down my mother's cheek. Both are fluent in the language of grief. The TV is on but nobody watches. My mother is hysterical. The baboon is by the cops, plucking their guns off like bugs. The house is a rotting fruit. The anchorman tells no one listening, Breaking news: we are all transplants in the wrong body. Too soon, I am smoke swallowed by the sky, nowhere.

Pig Flesh

I don't fuck with pigs like asalamalakum
—NICKI MINAJ

At lunch, we push loud and glaring titles in the scrollbar

> not sure what we're searching for,
> our desires tip-toeing.

But maybe we'll find it in one of these fisted
faces. In someone's hot voice that sings

> itself a verge, and hope to be forgiven
> after the echo dies. We were never

given the language to say *self* or *pleasure* or—
a shaykh says holding your own body

> is like eating the flesh of a pig
> to survive from major starvation

when no other food is available. Should we
sleep in a crypt? Should we cut off

> our own hands? Then the Khalīl
> Jubrān fairy enters my head. He says

I am like the boundless drop in a boundless
ocean, a tree heavy-laden with fruit

> that I may gather and give back
> to myself. I believe everyone.

Nothing satisfies the scavengers, too starved
for too long. You know what it looks

> like: snout-mucked swine, hunks
> of forbidden fat, and we are hungry

21

for flesh, to suck the scuz from our split hooves,
              limbs swaddled into a porky thicket, let

                                        the rot bloom us clean. I am alive
                                        writing this poem because

a jido didn't have his oil spilled and stolen without
              defiance, which has other ways of entering my life

                                        like in the Taco Bell parking lot,
                                        sliding off hijabs for a second—

Pakistani's a long straight tide, Sudanese
              a curtain of braids. These days I am never

                                        sure if my tears come from the
                                        come from the come from the God

come from the longing gut or I've been staring
              at artificial ice pixels for too long. Keep

                                        searching. *What's the holiest
                                        thing you've ever seen?* Girls

talk over each other between meat-warm threats
              to dabiha: *My grandma's hands. A dove's*

                                        *wings. Abdul's butt when he
                                        bends over to pray.* They are thinking

of dropouts working at their father's deli, calling out
              to us in Arabic when we step in for a snack.

                                        Their thoughts a duplicitous
                                        corner, pipes filling our lungs

with Starbuzz Blue Mist, Sex on the Beach, rousing
the animal their bodies remember they are

when starved, spitting its inborn snort
into the musk. Look how she teeters

on tightropes, half-crunk, twirling into the plunge,
then coming up for breath a little less cruel.

The adhan goes off. We don't deny
its call, or the gunk of guilt God

dumps on our heads. Who is to say what holy is?
Mary's menstrual blood? The prophet's first

kiss? Adam and Eve's graceless
groping? I try to unlock my cleaved

subconscious: one side a mosque, the other
a gritty sounder of unfocused breaths roasting

the air. I can still smell the hogs
when my head turns left and right

in prayer, the hooves gathered, for now, in some wild distance.

Portrait of This Country

Kiss someone. God will rat
          you out. He'll deliver a dream
                    to your mom at midnight where she learns

                                        what you're up to, awakened
                              with prophetic visions of your sins.

She will bust your door in a rain
          of spark spittle, fireballs.
                    This would never have happened if we hadn't

                                        come to this unholy country.
                              This country blamed for every failure,

clash for freedom. But new land
          doesn't change what has been set.
                    Your book is already written. Your thread-thin

                                        soul chosen especially for you.
                              STAY ALERT: on campus, picture

your spinal cord shot, scattered
          barbells, eyelids blood-scruffed,
                    smelling like jitters and singed sulphur.

                                        You speed walk grasping
                              a bread knife some nights. Glance behind

buildings every six seconds, hijab
          a lighthouse, fulgent white flash.
                    Pretend to read signs, tie your shoe in case

                                        you spot the dull heat in another
                              man's hand. You are sweat-itchy, drunk

on fright, always ready to rabbit kick
　　　away from anywhere. Then a cousin,
　　　　　　sharp-slick whiz, hexing smile. Killed

　　　　　　　　　　　　　　at nineteen, a hit-and-run on his own
　　　　　　　　　　front yard. One more mother stands quiet

by a window, too afraid to move.
　　　Each fajr, she turns the radio dial
　　　　　　as if searching for a certain song—

　　　　　　　　　　　　　a medium scanning for the dead.
　　　　　　　　　Gnawed ripe, breath-starved, throbbing

albatross: they are rough husks
　　　hauling their bellies through crowds
　　　　　　at groceries, ATM lines, waiting to become

　　　　　　　　　　　　another dark absence, another bleeding
　　　　　　　　hub. All of them still plagued by the uncle

in Yemen who never made it back
　　　from the market, ten years missing.
　　　　　　A neighbor's kid singing his last tune

　　　　　　　　　　　　on the school bus. Her daughter
　　　　　　　　kidnapped by the night. Yet all still agree,

This would never have happened, O
　　　this country ruined　　our children

　　　　　　their ruin　　is our ruin　　this country

　　　　　　　　　　is our children

　　　this ruin
　　　　　　is our country

                    is this

                              our ruin
    is this

              our country

                                        is this

حين يشقى الناس
When People Are Cursed

by Abdullah Al-Baradouni

You bemoan all, tired of never receiving eulogies
except in the speeches of your enemies.

أنت ترثي كل مَحزون ولم
تلق من يرثيك في الحطب الألَدّ

And myself, O my heart, I cry from the deepest part
of my eyes whether the tragedy is near or far.

وأنا يا قلب أبكي إن بكت
مقلةٌ كانت بقربي أو ببعدي

I have resolved to work hard to live rather
than continue crying for other's misfortunes all the time.

وأنا أكدى الورى عيشاً على
أنّي أبكي لبلوى كل مُكد

When people are cursed, I become miserable with them.
When I am doomed like them, I suffer with my misery alone!

حين يشقى الناس أشقى معهم
وأنا أشقى كما يشقون وحدي

I seclude myself to reflect.
Everybody is with me and my wealth.

وأنا أخلو بنفسي والورى
كلهم عندي ومالي أيّ عِندي

I do not need the material life, never have I had anything from it.
The only happiness is in the darkest night and I am drained.

لا ولا لي في الدّنا مَثوى ولا
مسعدٌ إلاّ دُجا الليل وسهدي

I do not trek from place to place like a refugee
only to feel punished, wearier.

لم أسر من غربة إلاّ إلى
غربة أنكى وتعذيبٍ أشدّ

I am exhausted. I walk mindlessly with my feet.
The sorrow is my food, the cold fever my clothing.

متعَبٌ أمشي ورُكبيّ قدمي
والأسى زادي وحُمّى البرد يُردي

The darkness is my mattress and my cover.
My body is overheating, my veins, my skin.

والدّجا الشاتي فراشي وردا
جسمي المحموم أعصابي وجلدي

Feast, Beginning w/ a Kissed Blade

She comes from a farm down south. But it's how she's butchered that's important,
 not where she's from. In our Yonkers garage, wet heat, naked air, everyone's elbows
 knocking. Her tongue itchy-pink as my Eid dress.
  We do it like in the bilad—headlocked & frothed
   w/ sweeteners, silver blade smooched w/ a bismillah,
    gullet sliced w/ thanks, w/ prayer. The lamb gasps.
   My uncles yank hard to tear her pelt, white fluff
     snowing our stratosphere. Same time last year, I walked onto a bus in Aden fully garbed & still
      got pawed, still *Lahm shabab*, blessing of young meat. They sing for her as she's strung, tongue
       limp, unfurled. Big body swinging thick, dripping
        blood the cats lick. Some leaks through the crack,
         a jogger prepped to call the cops on his crazy neighbors.
       We share & eat her all week: kebab skewed on bamboo,
         stewed w/ maraq, boiled as broth for the babies who forget
           the taste of pb&j, mac & cheese. Ribs noshed to needles. We pluck her from our teeth
            for the extra memory. I swallow my share w/ a Wolverine frenzy, taste my uncles'
             hands sifting through her like pearlers at the sea's
              bottom, the gentle way they pull out purple-blue
               strings, glimmering glut, until only an empty mollusk
                remained. How does one unlearn gorging? Fat fingers
                 pillaging piece by dutiful piece—Abraham, arms
                  raised, ready at the altar? We dress in sluiced lambskin, the dismembered carcass.
                   Eyes a salty snack. Her hooves high-grade handles. Juicy pulp called tongue saved
                    for dessert, that the men say tastes sweetest.
                   Here, w/ them, is where I learn of appetite—
                    to savor the innocent, to crave for the dead.
                     They teach me to bite life's head off, eat
                      my desires raw, let the spine of a slow
                       creature prick down & relish it. Here
                        is where I learn about the insides,
                         how to open w/ a varnished grace.
                        We skin the wild bull, wear
                          its leather on our chests.
              Feather the wrangled quail
              like a quick weeded field.
                    & when we slash
                     throats, we don't
                      look into their
                       glaring eyes,
                        don't ask
                         forgive-
                          ness.

٢

Hunger Wraps Himself

       with bandages, hobbles into a hospital
in Yemen like a zombified mummy

and bombs it—
       the cidal in lieu of scarcity. Magnesium echo.

Have the people ever told you what else they felt

when the underworld let out its minacious burp?
       Now they are wary of the space a body occupies.

Women dab themselves in rosewater,
                 become a fajr

of primal mumbling,

       prayers inconclusive in their grips.

Emptiness throws on a thermite gown
and enters a crowd. War waifs fight wild dogs

       for what remains.
Hope—Darwish's incurable

malady. I see it when my cousins turn to me,
       plates beaming their faces rapturous.

The motherland is ironed flat: unclaimed
edges, hand-dug wells, a grandfather's

skeleton. I peel the skin off everything,
even the grapes. I want to bend my neck

below a faucet for the gush that isn't bottled
or boiled, every sip cool, American, blessed

by God. In the souk are dragon trinkets,
painted sand, raw supplications to bring back,

place on a nightstand, say I was here.
Aunties crease in dark corners. Left alone,

they grow a fungus. I give one's daughter
the bruised banana in my bag. She kisses

her fingertips and taps them to her heart.
I note closely the footprint and fragrance

she leaves. Soon, she will dwindle to a gentle
zephyr, a nostalgic pang that ghosts this street.

All these kids tapering back to the mind
who made them. There, Allah will give

their stomachs solace and shish-kebabs.
Thi khalaqah razaqah. I buy a man a foil

of lamb dumplings. He returns half, says,
We don't eat to be filled. We eat to not go

hungry. I want to forgive the word devour,
cheeks qat-stuffed with grape leaves, Baba

at the table saying, *Less, habibti, less.*
Who finishes each grain we abandon.

Who used to mash grass into soggy bread
to stretch it. We show love through our appetite.

Famine happens when we can't remember our
name, the village we come from. I want to deserve

eating. An Arab who can't eat has lost control
of their heart. What can a girl learn from her cravings

once the begging gut goes quiet? By now,
she has grown intimate with starvation, wears it

like a pink buttercup behind her ear, handpicked
by a shy boy, later lost in the nest of her curls.

Guide to Gardening Your Roots

after Natalie Diaz

١

Somewhere, a brittle border, invaders packing the streets, *like when British colonizers came,* my father says, *reinventing us.* Yemen halved, and I with my neck beneath a grandmother as she parts my hair like Moses.

The British called us *El Bab*, the doorway. We are the entrance, our Red Sea the saltiest mother of waters. She is algae-thick, turning her copper as they die. The word *cure* was first birthed in her waves—us floating farhaneen, chalky castoffs who were once wreckbound and rumpused. This is our best medicine.

Alaietiqad hu alyamaniu, wa'ana alyamaniu is a Yemeni's faith thundered to their palms. *Belief (iman) is Yemeni, understanding (fiqh) is Yemeni, wisdom (hikmah) is Yemeni, and I am Yemeni.*

I have never been an opening to anything. My fatiha is still searching for the hands who will incision the earth and scatter me.

٢

There is a little village evading map lines, erased by riots, sharp tacks, the intangible wilderness. There is a half-constructed home of cinder slabs. A family clumps inside like ants in a drop of honey, sacred sticky resin. And they are happy.

Yemen of panthers and pillaring date palms. Of my great-aunts before dawn, squatting around the oven outside, molding dough into bread, scattering old bones to stray beasts, the musk of woodsmoke and haya.

Yemen dons haya obovata everywhere. The plant does not stop—it grows in even the dry parts.

Hayat in Arabic is to respect the self, which is to respect my forest, my mountain, my wells. We wear the حياة, too: seeded pods in our centers, defiant green tufts stretching through the sand.

I carry it inside me wherever I go, it is who I am.

Yemen faded in homespun photos, and Ratha's kids have been hungry, the market overrun, Ahmed beaten and captured from his car.

I come to the well to drink and find it living and thirsty itself. It drinks me. I drink it. And that is haya.

٣

What your TV doesn't tell you: my Baba can crack pistachio shells between his teeth and in the same motion flick them with his tongue into a bin ten feet away.

Summer, bugs bite valleys on our bodies, seeking a Yemeni's honeyed blood, thicker and sweeter than any.

We believe medjool dates can restore the soul.

I believe our noses are like hawks' beaks that grow longer when we smile.

٤

On the news, an eight-year-old American girl visiting Yemen dies from a raid approved by the president.

Nawar—her name, a flower. Was she seen as Yemeni or American? Did her real self exist in each?

Some days one flag blows more strongly than the other and it feels too much like betrayal. Some days the only choice is to grab everything and flee, graft your branches onto another tree. Start again.

I was never taught how to touch my dead. I look for a hole to hold her loose roots. Red on my hands and both of our flags.

I don't bother to cross-examine my accents. When I land, each country looks outside their windows and sees a fire-breathing invasion. I tell myself, as an American, I am not bound to just one land. I can taste a soldier's finger across the ocean as it caresses a trigger, its black tonsil.

Afterwards, it rains. I keep digging.

٥

Life, and all that lives, is conceived in the heart of the Yemeni. Haya is honor, born from the Arabic word for life. When you remember hayatna, you remember us.

Khalīl Jubrān wrote, *The breath of life is in the sunlight and the hand of life is in the wind.*

When my father says, *You sneeze you lose*, what he really means is, *Don't wait too long or every opportunity will pass by.*

When he says, *This light heavy*, what he really means is, *The sun is in my breath, each inhale a swallowed flame in my chest, and I am engulfed.*

The Yemen in my father treks years ahead of his life. Nothing is ever truly interpreted.

When someone حرق قلب, hurts a Yemeni from within, we are burned, a literal scalding to our hearts.

These days a Yemeni's heart cannot keep up its pumping, for faith and what faith manifests when starved.

What does hayati mean if my world is a desert, desolate, nothing but an empty blazing? If life is a rose-hued phantom circling the sand, what is the Yemeni?

The country snicked my father's heart. The hole gushes, *Because there are no more green fields and citrus trees. Now it's nothing and I'm from nowhere.*

What should I have said to him then? Maybe: *Search for a new sun whenever the blood spills*, or, *I wish you hadn't told me.*

٧

The prophet ﷺ said, *The people of Yemen are on the verge of ascending upon you as if they are clouds.*

I plant our spangled plotlines in tin canisters, tempt a flower to rocket out, offering myself as witness.

No healing exists beneath the ground after a burial. But haya grows in an empty desert. The implication being that water trickles back to its center. That even the unrooted can ascend.

Operation Restoring Hope

\

Death doesn't choose who it favors. A missile does.

It might go for the last field of melons.
Or a front gate the uncles just painted, white
as bonefish, its tips reaching the lowest

heaven. It can choose the funeral, kill one hundred forty,
wound five hundred more.

There is no time for mourning. The people of Yemen are tossed
back into the cage without ceremony.

It might choose the mountain
girl, a break in her brother's shepherd stick
where the corpse fell.

Now she is the sister of ruin, knows what an eyeball does
when dazed, full of exile.

The ghaltan who pressed the launch button wishes
he were a blade of grass a beast eats
so that he is not accountable for anything.

Forgiveness will not be found in this stretch of desert.
No, a mother does not cover her child's eyes
when violence comes. When his body is lassoed

into the fray, a blameless hummingbird
cannons out. Its beak babbles. Its wings gleam
a green sunrise. Not long now until baladi is missiled
inside out, my people swallowed into its silence.

٢

A restored body looks like the opposite of men
wearing matching shirts, marching in formation.

A body restored looks like the other version
of a child dusted in camouflage. The restoration

of a body is the antonym of a rolling river,
which is a river dried, which is a thirst
to forget everything ever taught about death.

How many corpses until the atfal of Yemen learn
that no lion lives in the throat of their cries?

The first hope was no bigger than an eyelash,

was born in the middle of war, where we were told prayer
can change the fate of anything. Even dirt.

If you repeat an impossible wish over and over,
does it become a prayer? Illa. For what
is prayer but the expansion of our hopes
into the living ether?

Someone's daughter hopes to be lifted by her Baba,
hopes to break her fast each morning,
for a few minutes to play ball with the boys. She bobs

unfutured with the waves of the Red Sea, water salted
with blessings.

We operate on the spirit of this country like doctors
with no training. We hope for change

but don't know which cave it hides in, waiting for a hero
to find and bring back to us.

I imagine Allah as ever-shifting. As light
that keeps dazzling. As a low hum in the throat

of a boy soldier, his mother's lullaby a solace
as he toes around the landmines, still humming to himself
when the fragments hit.

The mountain girl tries to stay sane
after grief. She talks to her sheep,
its one ear cocked forward to listen.

Enter, a Yemen of zaman: kids chasing blue
and pink lizards. A mother leaning from her window
to rain cool water over them. Heads lustered

with tahimi hats, henna trees slopping
bright dyes. One swing in the center of the village
to feel the hawk's flight, of roped wood
wa whatever chains they could find. Folk singers,

qanbūs strings, milyan shukr and music in the middle
of hayi—there's a wedding in the hood
and everyone and their khala is invited,

where a trigger is pulled only in celebration, gun
shot from the highest hilltop, bulleting the sky.

Yemen Rising as Poorest Country in the World

Ruling Yemen is like dancing on the heads of snakes.
—EX-PRESIDENT ALI ABDULLAH SALEH

This country like a pan of maa'tuf crisped
too dark. This country at the map's edge like a scrunched

fist. This country a trading port, a locust flying full speed,
a jinn queen, a pleasant resonant, a goggle of glimmering

noses. This country who invites the whole village
over for tea is a blue diwan, a spice road, an Arabia Felix.

Yemen of wadded cheeks, feral cat and snake fights.
A hen walking into your kitchen, kids outside chasing

the cock who chases fajr. This country of spiffed grandmothers
in gaudy galabeyat dancing to the beat of their own heartdrum

as they wait on the long line for petrol. This country is a canal
between al nas and the divine. It is suit jackets draped over thobes,

jambiya blades at the waist. Or rahman in a tucked foutah,
squatting at the knees to eat. This country is a dwindled

miswak, a line of red teeth chomping down the bark
of the kingdom. A Yemeni will not fear the hereafter,

busy carrying jerry cans of water from an aid camp
miles away. The water here is weaponized. The water here

is full of parasites and pirates. If you swim too long,
either one can steal you. The politicians that dug themselves

into our fields were bad seeds. They sprouted only
the poisonous parts, left the best of Allah somewhere else.

National Unity Day was yesterday. I lit a sparkler
that looked like the worms on my cat's ass, white

electric, wriggling where I waved it. Baladi is twins
wrestling for separation in the womb, the two linked

through blue cord and brain folds. The north came out
hot as lightning and just as striking, the south's head

a beautiful gleaming coffeeberry. One tries to reach
the other's border, calling out their birth name

through the divide. اسمعني. The prophet ﷺ once said
the people of Yemen have the softest hearts of all.

I've been trying to ensnare you in your own guilt.
I never aimed for liquid speech. I should have been

more rhetorical. Maybe someday I'll push
the language of poor through my mouth and master it.

Coffee Arabica as a Maelstrom of Endless Aftershocks

Kaldi the goat herder found his flock prancing
                    near our bush. And so flung a few bulbs
                              into himself. The sudden gong in his chest—

orchestral surge, dried delirium. He named our tree
                    gahwa, *force*. The sun can't scorch our petal-
                              wax. Cut the axils and we spread faster, a cluster

of glossy evergreens. Stretched by field children
                    for ice cream, pinched for a cousin's flu.
                              To speed a mother's labor, swift-born baby slippery,

red-faced, smelling of something sweet. Jasmine
                    takes hostage your nose. Black potion arranges
                              the fajr. With each bow, our aroma trills

your brain with coffee logic: visions of robbed
                    caskets, your mother's eyes at the mug's bottom,
                              of sacrament, obsidian gleam, angels melting

from the roof like snow. It is no good to want
                    for restlessness. Force alone can't ford the river.
                              We will help you forget yesterday, walking past kids

huddled in nests of flimsy boxes, soot-cheeked.
                    How the youngest dodged cars, scaled bricks
                              to reach you, tugged her torn pants down

for the coins you carried. *Haqq al qahwa*, she said.
                    You stood rolling around the tempest linger
                              from your breakfast cup as the morning trembled

on the ground before you, wanting to cry tears
                    of qahwa to gift her. Which classic roast
                              will canter you out of your travesties, burning

as you harpoon it down? These days you grow
    your spine with the sound of our brewing.
        What of halawa? What of the stout sugar cube

you claim to be? You recently hooked an allergy
    to caffeine, and to the exposure of desperation.
        As if fears come to life in drinking them.

As if the surge our berries bring could trip you.
    You keep us in your diet, but keep the dead
        at arm's length. Your ghosts are choking

on our titterful vapors, begging for a final taste,
    to be buried in a pile of our bounty,
        whole graves waking up like Lazarus

when we touch their careful bodies. You are so
    so tired. Nothing roots you in an instant
        like we do. Wings grow after the first sip

and you can't give up this flight. Look at yourself.
    Here are my blissful biceps, here are my
        sunburnt teeth. One gulp and already dressed

in shudders. We are the constant niggle, the first
    to dance and last to sleep. We live in the prayer
        between your lips. There is only so much of us,

the land a bed for the qat, both of our leaves holding
    a blood-locked energy. So when the wind drops
        our withered white togas on your path, consider it

divine droppings. He who so collects a handful
    will be love letter, will be slaked treaties.
        And on another side of the country, one of us

is ripening, is soon to be
                    split

               in half, crushed of all its gahwa.

The Snapping Turtles in Ta'iz Have Beards

Our elders say eating lahm wa zanjabil soup smeared
with the stain of a forefather can spark the snapping turtle

to strike. And if you can't prevent it, may as well
keep quiet when webbed hands push you into a wall and say

I want to rape you. Don't bother crying or asking him
to consider you like his son. A boy before you tried that.

The beak just bit harder and a rifle came out. In Arabic,
the word for son is ibn. Someone's ibn is tricked.

Look at him, so small and filled with forgiveness.
The door closes. Sandals crushed down in the back

abandoned between the wisteria vines. Don't worry.
As the turtle undresses his shell, the boy shoots him

with his own gun, then bolts with his panic. Sure,
his turtle friends slash the boy's whole family

(turtles have sharp feet, hooked jaws). But hey, at least
the cage has stopped rattling. In Arabic, the word

for rape is also for disgrace, is also for ravishment.
Forget about the knife, the fork, the pinch of salt.

The famished turtle has had his soup. The flavors
of misery it summoned made him hungrier. Your foreign

turtle calls you pretty angel, asks if you love this country.
Unfortunately, the reptiles stationed in Ta'iz have beards

to muffle this hairy situation. Saudi-backed militiaturtles
scan the market for a boy trout's secret marrow, the invaded

privacy of the flayed, prized out with a pick and swallowed.
Your mother reporting the bite won't do anything.

They will ask for forensics, but the doctor is under Islahi turtle
control. He will demand report money she can't pay. He is not afraid

of God. Do you see where this is going? A mother of Yemen
will lean over your dish and fill it, and when you finish,

fill it again. Tell her to give it up. You stay empty
and infected, the star student who can't hold a pen

stirring in your own jim-jams, wake up screaming.
Personally, I'm against eating little boys. I'm just saying

what's already in the books. The *Journal of Politics* wrote
gang rape is used as a means of bonding among turtle

soldiers. They break bread together, sop your shame
with a piece of khubz. You wallow in the salacious earth

covered in his algae, waiting to be dug up by faithless strays
who look you in the eye, see you as one of them.

One longs for a rectum with retractable fangs. For a country
not castled in conflict and absent laws. Our elders warn only

the daughters about the street of hard shells and bony
beaks, forget about abna'ona. Don't get me wrong—

turtles like the taste of flowers, too, (they are omnivores
and very dynamic with their assaults, I mean meals). Worry

not. The daughters are safe at home heating up the country's
soup. Into the pot: four garlic cloves, five dried jujubes, carnage

of petals. Find her in the kitchen sweeping table crumbs
and trepidation from the floor once everyone has had their fill.

Dream Interpretation [*Fox*]

Found napping in your purse means you will bump into your younger self trekking through a botanical garden, searching for an apology.

A tail plucked and pinned to your hijab means an uncle will beg you to marry his son, bring him across the ocean where he won't know hunger.

I can't stop eating, even the spines—they shred my throat, tongue a raw copper. I have stopped apologizing with intention. Get myself a triple cheeseburger, bacon this time. Very American. Because that's what I am now, right? Tripping over familiar shapes on an empty road, dizzy from the shisha and the pork, thinking headlights look holy from afar. How easy to make a thing all wrong. Most of my cousins are dying. The littlest leads me by the hand into a cave streaked with limestone, handprints, a swollen matriarchy. I find our famished ancestors cooking beside orange tatters. In their circle, a fox, her body ready for the fire.

at the summit, he finds a nest

qat has hindered the country's progress, the national narcotic leaving damaging effects on
yemen's health and society. —AL JAZEERA

after danez smith

\

boys chew in the bark dust, buzzing red-
toothed, rapturous. like their babas, they brave

for nothing but their birth tribe. so what
if they slip small glories in their pockets?

boys chew and chew and chew until
those gold hills become unbearable.

the carnelian grass hiding a man's
penance. they spit crimson globs

and god, *ptwey*, scorch-ready, waiting
for their country to glitch, glamour out,

evolve into the emirate. where else
could surahs have cackled if not from

the mouths of men, jummah fantasia
in their bellies? brothers dodge stones

and their genesis being called from a pillar.
he isn't afraid to dig deep inside his flesh

palace for spunk, heroic nerve. boys
learn they must walk down the street,

meet eyes with the soldier on the corner
before they can face a father. that a leaf

is just a leaf, through all its tiny veins.
that a baba   is just a baba.

                    ٢

drugged land. drugged blood. drugged
years that drool out boys innominate
with the heat waves, tree-brown

          and fat-cheeked. it helps them forget
                    the burns on their foutahs, the green
                    casket of a cousin they just carried.

they can't find the tunes that sung them
lawless, the shepherd that calls off war.
wasn't it yesterday they were loitering

          in their father's beards, prickling
                    themselves into his rituals?
                    all yemenis are loved because

your very veins are a virtue.
they catch prophethood
thrashing mid-air.

          they make wudu with the dirt
                    on their hands. they swear
                    oaths with their souls.

                    ٣

if you enter a sniper's hole
          you can smell the bottom of a lake.
                    one floating dead fish and other
                              gilled relatives. a crack-tongued boy
                                        fills a bowl to drink from, his bowl overflowing
                                                  with rot. look how a boy sniffs his way
                                                            out of a black cave. the shooter's marks
                                                            are reborn as shadow arms that try

                                        to hug their boy to the walls,
                                          wet with missing.
                                        he lets them. this
                                        is his history.
history burns his nostrils a little.
        a little wind speed goes a long way
                for the sniper, who calculates distance
                        and the decades it will take to fill an empty
                                well. there are boys still hugging while holding
                                        their breaths. yemen's odor makes him retch.
                                                the scent of his mother's abaya revives him.

                ع

in the sky, buzzards wait for boys in battle
to drop. in the tobacco, farmers beg

for clean water. tiny feet crunch
the confetti they get high on. a bird

of yemen will snatch anything:
hijab, clothespin, a baby. an egg

falls. a bird that plucked itself naked
falls after it. stray cats eat them.

nests drip down. boys try to hold them
all, their parts unravelling. sometimes

he catches thorns, scrap metal, a dank
jersey of america's. sometimes he seized

an olympian existence, beeswax leading
up to safety. his wings: qat-slog, gutted

glue, a father's hands suturing his son
into an outline of escape. the boy

flies towards the sun, not melting.
he makes a new house on its light beam.

he slings good news into everyone's window.
the birds become his brothers who feed him.

◊

at the summit, he finds a nest.
in every corner a mosque, a kingdom,
a grandfather's lap. funerals don't
exist. the petals chime lullabies
when plucked. the shrubs hold
an uncle's blessing, not cud.
everyone's gums bulge only
with caramel contentment,
halawa hewing. boys catapult
shoeless into a fresh strophe,
a sidr-sweet version
they return to. one without
the beating herons, or the hunger.
at the summit, there is always
noor. if he listens hard, he can hear
the sun speak. she tells him,
those scars you called home
will cream over. she says,
if you find a feather glowing
on the ground, wrap it
in your waist and keep it.

Hidden Bombs in My Coochie

١

my accent not arab enough
to haggle   people know I'm not native
from my swaying
flux   in the city of brick slabs
the lost nipping your heels
for a soft touch
an outlaw asks where home is
finds it funny when I say *demmi yemeni*
I board the plane back
to my birthplace   sturdy
blue proof in my pocket
alien again when I land

٢

I sing two anthems
squeeze a moshed lineage
in every boxed foyer
I walk   baba still speaks to me
in arabic   but we listen
to britney spears   watch family feud
remind ourselves of yemen
with the khubz as utensil
when we kiss cheeks
in odd numbers   remember
a grove's perfuming
before the marooned onslaught
when children didn't play
the game with charcoal & cotton
called   who can make
gas masks the fastest

٣

when I step outside
violence becomes a rising

of my neck hairs   running
through a murky two-lane
out of breath so I don't end up
like bambi's mama shot dead
in my tracks   I can't say
I never saw it coming
curled fetal in a forest
caucasian man's bullet in this
dumb blah brain   my small son
waiting in a tree's shadow for me
to surge up from the tall grass
nudge his wet dark nose
with my nose

ع

in america I am automatic:
towelhead & hidden
bombs in my coochie
ass fat for that Isis
dick 9/11 suss lookin'
bitch that sandy toed
camel fucker cousin fucking
to make more terrorist
babies a fourth wife
mia khalifa in a burqa
lookin' bitch long rifle
nose from your uncle
bin laden lil' bitch

٥

amreeka settles my body
into place   it unbends
the flick of my wrist
when I talk   turns
my femurs into fire escapes
eyes canonized chasms
my neck's axis craning

down   it tells baristas
my name is tina
tongue ebbing far away
from me
the news makes me believe
I was born to cock
back this rifle sleek & steady
like a true terrorist the news
makes me want to grab
my phone & gun
it out the country
the news makes me touch
myself   find the panic
button of my body
& press hard

Home Security After 9/11

💣 *Consent: if the police show up at your door and ask you if they can come inside to search and you consent to the search, then the police do not need a warrant.*

At the break of moon, a front door Herculesed
to pine dust, children dreaming of [   ].
Forced from sleep,

dogs shepherd us into a nightened cave
where a mother is crying, *Let me grab a scarf, just a scarf.*
Bleary-brained in its meteor glow, static shouts belling
the block, I believe

we are being abducted by [   ].
I ask the low white light, *Where will all the Muslims go?*
Blue men bustle me into their van, everything a slow
lucent swing, lashed stiff in this effigy. An old blister

bursts. Blood sieges
the street in a crucible of war.
It pummels the god-prince. It pleads for [   ].

💣 *Plain view: police do not need a search warrant to seize evidence that is in plain view of a place where the police are legally authorized to be.*

Hours later, escorted inside for some Reese's Puffs
before school, "Number One Dad" mug
in a behemoth's hands.

A maggot nibbles through my nostril
as I munch, the violent violation. "Red Nation" rises
from a radio, Lil Wayne plopping *Tough luck* into my
breakfast bowl. *Pour me*

another cup you filthy [   ],
the behemoth snarls through the cage of his teeth.
I do it when he shifts, shows his [   ], shiny as
a scourge of blood, says, *This right here*

is your Allah.
             How many moments like these
seared into my timeline, unchangeable as 9/11?
I am aware
             of many things: the softening cereal,
my paper-thin lungs. That there is no boundary
of [   ] in a body.

🍒 *Is the person whose home or property being investigated/searched expected a degree of privacy? Was that expectation objectively reasonable? I.e., would society as a whole agree that the place or thing should remain private?*

It would seem the exits want to keep vanquishing.
We hunch in corners, untraceable breaths.
The trees

                tribute us for our stillness—
Muslims with a cityscape, shots ringing,
a trespasser older than time in their chests.
Did they hear

                          my aunt sobbing over tapped
phones on her way to buy lahm as the towers [   ]?
Are you close to the [   ]? Is there a lot of [   ]?
Anyone listening?

We find flags
                tooth-picked between our frames of the kaaba.
Each one whips a firework heat, red-blues consecrating
along our skin, smoke in our mouths, American touch.

My father gets a home-security system—darklarge
pupils always watching. *Just in case*, he says.
We speak in [   ],
                    afraid they bugged the rooms,
imagining a device that hunts our [   ].
My parents
                    turn down the music, lock the kids up,
place trackers in every car. I fall asleep with my ears:
growling K9s, laughter in the kitchen, click of a [   ].

My President Asks Me about Redemption

a found poem: Khalīl Jubrān's The Prophet

Then a president said, Speak to us of Redemption.
  And the poet answered saying:
  Absolve by mopping your bitter poison off the streets. Watch it flow purple out our living rooms.
  For to be redeemed is to girdle the people's agony.
  And to not fasten it around your America, now empty and dark.

You told yourself, Hell is nothing more than an opening, so you slept peacefully.
  And always you have been told that redemption is the dust on the path to power.
  But I say to you, suck the thickened venom from your wound.
  Spit it on a Muslim's prayer rug, where it turns into a goat tasked with ramming horn-first into
your noggin, tackling your demons.

For redemption exists in healing yourself. Thus, your people.
  Let me be clear.
  You plucked us like lizards out a crevice for dinner.
  Left a man begging by the saguaro, eating sand, crying, I'm hungry, I'm hungry.
  Where are his children who learned to never call the cops or they'll point the wrong finger?
Who watch the moon's tilting across the border?

The poor may speak to you of emptiness, but he cannot give you his hunger.
  The refugee may speak to you of leaving, but he cannot give you his drowned.

Which of us would be another murmur on this block? Another dimmed gangsta faced with
  death?

And I say, redemption is a golden glade above your head.
  In its light, you see the people for what they could have been—a friend, a cousin, a warm
greeting through peaceful streets that said,
  Brother, join me for a minute on the stony porch with the old tabby, a tray of tea.

Call redemption a shape-up for the soul. Call it by your barber's name. Call it by your
neighbor's.

Often seen you at the park, poking at the ladies, pleased by their quivering.

Often heard you say, as if speaking in sleep, Make America great.

I say, not in sleep, but in the over-wakefulness of noontide—here is the horse and here is the arena.

We are still here, we will always be here, we, the dirt under the nails of your country, crusted red from digging.

God rests in the distant fields, waiting.

٣

Heritage Emissary

As designated translator, I taste saffron, gold coins,
a slight burning. Since I've returned, there has been less

of me in English. Though *return* always meant measuring
the earth's door, tongue ozoned and still learning

to stretch between here and home. Sah, my native
speech is like a window sash pulled up wa down.

Sah, I shift phrases without thought. Classmates tilt
at my returned self like I grew horns, can shoot bombs

out my ass. Like they want to dump me in ma'a,
watch me float like a witch. When I Arabic my way

towards them, they pat my back in case I hack mucus
wa dem. What do you call a word the mouth has forgotten

to push out, stuck by the tonsil's entrance, squirming
to be sound? Speech becomes a slagged pot I bang crude

beats on. I long to play a song that doesn't terrorize,
a song that's understood. The mushkila is I am a surging

current of feared language. Words have stopped arriving
easily. Was it Rumi who said silence is the language

of God and all else is poor translation? I am not
mithluhum. I can't properly translate myself,

                    part I hush tongue my floats lake settled a so
              need I steam senseless of shrouds spout and lips my

          don't I proof need I with accent my sink to dictionary a
          .sense make still can I that cooing blurred a like sound

I lie about my D in Algebra. Turn, *She daydreams*
during lessons into, *Qaluu I pay attention to detail.*

Turn, *She's suspended for fighting* into, *I'm such a good*
student, they gave me a day off. Each rephrasing

Pinocchios my nose. I am out of breath from so much code-
switching, crunching the sand it leaves my teeth.

When threatened with a call home, I shrug, *Taib.*
Go ahead. They'll say, yes yes, *but won't yafhumun,*

will ask me about it later so I can twist it. At dinner,
Baba tells a story of his childhood in Yemen.

About catching a wild fox with his cousin—Arabic
the medium through which his body can return home.

I drown him out. Ana asif, I don't mean to. It's only that
my languages get mukhtalita, and when he talks it sounds

mithl poetry. So when I hear a line about a lost,
sly animal, I am struck mute. Think he means me.

I Thicken the Room w/ Dim Mirrors & an Altar of Aliens, Waiting for a Sign

Charged & marbling, Baba flies w/ me, shows me where he grew up & I
alien my way into his country to make it mine—bury my lashes in the dirt,

guzzle its rapid A'rabi. When my mother met him for the first time, she thought
alien & sewed her citizenship into her hijab. But then they slow danced on a balcony,

spinning their yellowed papers, an angel playing their flute. In Baba's language,
alien sounds most like stranger, like no community. In Yemen, I loved sharking

the tall mountains, twining my hair w/ hawk bones. Then a cousin said, *Ukhti, watch me
alien this bullet w/ a soaring brain.* I catch its falling feathers w/ my teeth. My hands

serpent the wind's exit wound. He says practice is a moltened survival. He is fluent in
alien. A fortune auntie tells my mother, *She will marry Yemen's ghost.* Like most in my house,

we smog our mirrors w/ what we deem fearless, swinging the heavy pendulum—bespelled
aliens who never return the same. Are we really meant to live forever shipwrecked,

drowning at the slash-throat edge? I didn't realize I was Arab until one afternoon on the
alien of September, while in Aden, escaping cars were strapped w/ duffel-bagged babies.

O unclaimed prayer, when will you cease sinking? I wonder if my mother made an
alien of herself for my father. She said she did it selfishly, countless nights of English

lessons in the kitchen so he'd no longer be a lack of shade in her life. In my veins, an infinite
alien. It runs thick. It runs naked, greased garnet, my darksparked fixture. I want to paddle

to remedy island, ask the panthers lapping my stranded blood, *Which part of me tastes most
alien?* I was a jellyfish before this body, slipping away when my mother spoke

to Avon customers on Lexington, who wore socks worth forty stomachs back home. If an
alien is splayed & dissected, an opal light will fall from its eye & victim that city. No security

guards remove the women off Lexington. None asks the other, *Where are you really
alien?* We forget Lady Liberty is flammable & foreign, corroding a petrified green. Her mirror,

our mirror. In it, the alien grimes. She alienates all other tongues.
The carbon moon path leads to a necklace of joy-armored aliens.

.it follow I

My Father Finds Home through the Birds

What did I know, what did I know
of love's austere and lonely offices?
—ROBERT HAYDEN

Pigeons on Broadway follow him like winged guards. He bargains
with a yard finch to peck us

      when we cuss. Someone's love birds let loose

         in the hood & my father calls them

with a whistled song, the soft clapping
of his heart. Along broken leaf light, he marvels a hawk's lonesome flight

into the emptiness, its feathered breast
a qibla. He can't trace his footprints.

      He still wants to belong, even after leaving.

   How does a Baba know when to remain, & when to unravel the nest?
He grew among the ancient zaytun his whole

      childhood, & see how they spill

         their oil on his arms

like an invasive species. I peck for something daughterful,
something that won't chip

      his teeth, leave seed pits

         in his shoes. I long to hang my homeland

on the wall, eat it like a beak hammering at bark, the violent
hunger. For someone to point me on a map, take their finger

& say, *Here she is.* Darwish wrote, *Words are a homeland.* So I bring my father
to listen to a white professor describe

the village his family comes from

to feel less alone. It's stunning, words I would wrap

in a gift box, place in front of his mother's prayer rug.
But somewhere in the bucolic, a cousin digging, ruby-throated, searching

for his leg. The neighbor, grass in her mouth, spit-
feeding her baby. Maybe it's how the man says *soil*, the way he uses crimson

to evoke our mud-brick homes.

Or maybe it's how he compares noon

reflecting off the mountain's fog to fire. My father's America
has a thicker mist

than those Yemen woodlands. My father's America has a glass window
where he sees someone like him,

flies forward too fast, concussed

& caught in the long wind.

I bite into olive stones to feel my Baba's migration.
I hurl them into ponds

the way Zeus hurls his bolts of jewel orchids, lamping the night.

There is a raptor collecting fox fur in his beak, held by
the sky like large, spectral

hands. Who decides to extend

into that deafbarren gap, but the thing

that wholly gives in? There is a submission in flying, in the wind
that gathers him, feathers splayed

      & begging the sky to grant

            just an eighth of its tribe to call his.

Dream Interpretation [*Sea*]

Placed at your feet means you will inherit a large amount of shoes that are not your size.

Walking into one fully garbed means you will drive someone dear to you out of your life.

Another burkini ban somewhere and over a hundred degrees, but women strip only their shoes. A few sit in the waves like ocean litter—glossy black bags tossed in and left to soak. I can't find my sandals. Nothing in this dream is my size. Even the water wraps too tight. Up to my mouth, dark as venom I want to suck into my lungs, lick the cool bottom. I don't care about the poison because I am thirsty, because I am already sick from the doubt. Someone I lost long ago paddles over, presses an apricot to my mouth. I taste a truce. Its juice drips down their fingers. To sink would be so easy.

After Running Away from Another Marriage Proposal

I'm not lonely, I'm alone. And I'm holy by my own.
—JAMILA WOODS

I run, for months a furred wind of sand and blue silt. At the dunes, midnight. I am in the mounds, illumed, topaz-mooned, sprinked quiet.

A rishta auntie's whisper falls out of a shooting star. My animal ear pivots, *To be single is to grieve. Until zawaj, you are only half of what you could be.*

Less than one body. Only a piece of complete. Made whole by someone else.

In another swift star, I hear Jubrān. *The silence of aloneness reveals to their eyes their naked selves, and they would escape.* Jubrān is wrong. The auntie, too. I celebrate my naked, lonesome self. Less escape, more journey, desiring nothing but to fill my own appetite.

Tyro to the desert, I mix impulse with inclination. I give things up to the dunes: cottontails, banquet of iron, lost shoes and licked bones, two burnished rings.

The fox stands heavy over my heart, watching the vast, empty valley, bronzed by the yellow moon.

Sometimes I believe the auntie. That I don't carry all of me—a lint blur, too translucent to be kissed, bristling arm hair the only thing giving me away.

Back before I was phantom smoke unspooling from a mouth, I would watch Arab Idol with my father. The only Yemeni group came on. Judges cried.

He phoned right then, *I just heard you sing. It reminded me of home.* They laughed and spoke, the singer not surprised to have a stranger find his number on Facebook, calling like a war-lost brother catching up.

What transpires in the sphere of familiarity? Do hands unabashed live inside it? Do they simply bubble out the circle, reaching, already magnetized to everyone? And which of those hands will coax the creature out of her dreamsome hills, remind her of the weight of the loving?

The hills are crowding. A coyote cries, quavering shrill, small throat searching for her mate, breaking the bedrock and my flesh, both gleamed open. Out leap brilliant sapphires I never knew I had, fully formed from the start, rouging and lightglossed.

My mother kneels in a lapis-dim room for a man to lift her daughter, scruff first, collared and declawed, to be set inside القفص الذهبي, the golden cage of marriage—howls hushed between bixbyite bars.

Before I knew the feel of a desert shade, I knew my mother. She wore her own fox once. Before my father, before the move, when she was a girl like me, and wanting.

In a country run by shaykhs and kings, she disrupted the barren land. Dressed in men's thobes with akhawatuha at the mall, behind the wheel of a car—diamond whole, spine whole,

spit whole, teal mud and mica-pawed. She moved as suns do, Helios with his chariot, her rays radiating anywhere she wanted.

Now she WhatsApp calls a khala to maunder about banat like me—*freeze eggs* a normal calendar memo, tickets to J-Cole instead of Suhaib Webb, all those shelter cats.

I, alone—in the quartzed dune, a fox elusive as water, out of reach without the right incantation, a supermoon.

The moon is not full, is not caviled for her halfness. She glows loudly. And her glowing says, *Go. Gnaw down to the amber. Tuff the gemmed lock to the ground. Become a storm-grown she-beast, glutted and content with your wholeness, with your fangs that work best against gold.*

I Crack an Egg

once against a porcelain bowl
  and out glops my mother dressed in runny
yellow, telling me when to cleanse Arab
  from the palate, if I salt too little,
how to eat like I'm deserving of love.

  I stand in her clammy kingdom,
bandana tight, cat begging by my feet. There are daughters
dropped at the mosque by mothers who bark,
  May Allah guide you and screech off.
  An imam finds them weeping, says, *Heaven lies*

under the feet of your mother, the sin of defiance
  like murder. Beneath my feet, the doomed
  kitchen, tiles that darken where I walk. Find a city
of mothers circling the block to be alone
  when they cry for our unscathed hands.

In the forge of her skull, a blacksmith hammers
  without rest. A mother tasked with survival might
miscarry the moon unnoticed. She is the cracked egg,
  yolk cradled back and forth between each shell,
  dragged out of her in a slow sway through the years
  until the clear is gone completely.

What did I really know about leaving the water?
  All I know is, if you dump a daughter
tied and gagged into the trunk of a car, make sure
  her mother is with her so that they may die together.
  I address my mother like a woman addresses

herself, bald-faced wa maftooh. When I was breathed
  into being, carnality came before the egg.
  There was a time we both were one base, body
  lobbing like a ball, her breath, my breath,

her blood a Nile passing two borders.
Did the pulse come first, or the battle
        splatter? I want to go back to that birth, choking
            on placenta, limitless, not yet like
the dirged women before me, regrets floating
        in a gray haze over my shoulder. I harvest

my mother, reap the badlands of her terrible limits,
            waiting for the rain. On my thirteenth birthday,
        we ran in dusty shib shib to the park behind Roosevelt
and buried my fox tail in red sand. *A smart girl
        can have her way in anything if she's slick enough.*

        She made me swear wallah with kul nafsi
that one day I would be a bride dhakia, a slippery
            sea urchin, the crafty creature
man shall never know about. I never saw her like that
        before, never have again: gutter flood
            of conviction, hijab sailing on a spike,
        cawing until crows torpedoed from the trees.

She muddied my cheeks. Showed me
            my constellation. Taught me codewords
        and how to dance with dark pythons.
        We were moth bitten, in full effect,
free as unhinged jaws, spin-drifting into clouds
        that bulged with a begging to flood.

He might be the head, but you're the neck,
        she said, crouched wild and eye level,
a booby-trap babe carved in moon ripples.
        That day I learned Arab women
are dangerous and beautiful witches, the smallest
    vertebrae, schemers holding secret control.

One night, I'll run back to that park and unbury
my high-risk. Bedouin women will vine swing
      from the shadows, swipe me from beneath
my mother's feet and spin me into an Aroosa.

      My lashes curled into scythes, bangles
made from bones, veiled with a rubied
      blessing. Their ululated hymns to me what an egg
sings when dropped, readying me as a mother
      would, boiled to stone hardness for this cruel dunya.
A daughter somewhere has committed murder.

It smells like a burning omelet.
Suddenly, her mother is there—there, scouring
      her hands raw with Brillo and stove fire,
whispering through the crunch of eggshell teeth,
      Don't mistake softness as something owed to you.

Middle Eastern Music

sounds like God blaring poems
like Fairouz not Madonna

            like dispossessed mouths

sometimes like sandy lashes
or rainwater dripping down

            bare breasts in a hammam

actually more like coin rattle
in a beggar's cup

            on a belly dancer's midriff

sounds like bombastic without
the bombs and sweat

            beneath a veil I swear it

sounds like a circus of siblings
as an auntie

            cusses you out

with over-doused atir on everyone's
khalu but at night it's

            your own blood stalking you

like a bored soldier
these days it's the sound of being

            in an airport combing

of suffering swept into a dustpan
with wrinkled tobacco leaves

            is that the music or

a drone whizzing above   listen
it sounds a little like

            a hijab fetish

incense and spice packets
a mother chanting *God forbid*

            God forbid   it is history

tidied up to sound better
and homework still

            riddled with bullet holes

yet some days it sounds like
Baba blasting WhatsApp videos

            in the living room

or your grandmother trying to convert
the neighbor's cat to Islam or   a cousin crying

on the phone where al hokuma
are always listening   except for   the sex worker's whisper

in Amran *After the rape I had*
no choice   it sounds   like the spling splang

of topazian teacups or
the spling splang   of swimming

from one busted boat straight
into another   can you hear   a khadama's passport

snatched as she hangs from
a fifth-story ledge   her employer   saying *I own you*

usually sounds like a sword's shriek
before the sheep's slaughter   but if you listen closer you can catch

bundles of bones bowing together
prayers softened with need and   sunrise   the adhan   all that weight falling

on clean ears   soundless until
the tongue takes on a new tune   who else is lost and lying full among the song?

Please Take Off Your Shoes Before Entering

for the massacred Muslims in Christchurch, New Zealand

the mosque little one / right foot first to dissipate

        the jinn / *shhh* while others pray / God is not

a game / people's bowed backs are not

playgrounds / Allah sees you sneak / to the shoe rack

to wear a stranger's sparkly sandals / tie knots to all the Nikes

        listen / Qur'an is being read as a euphonic

song / let it lullaby you / please no sliced bananas

on the prayer rug / do not giggle little Muslim monkey

it isn't funny / do not disturb the people / who find it difficult

to approach the angel smiling / please stop snaking your mother's

ankles / her face slipping somewhere else / dipped beneath

the surface of a stream / for your kidney donor / for the money

it will need / for no more drunk men / pulling her headscarf

        when she exits the subway / she scoops you

with one arm / puts you down when she prostrates

picks you up again / when she stands / laser-focused

mama / Incredible Hulk mama / mythos mama with

a million backbones / skin smelling of the sweet milk

you will only find again / when you're dead / in the fountain

        of paradise / please do not disturb these parents

on their knees / praying you won't give them heart attacks

leaving at night to play grown-up / in streets

that don't want you / please stay away / from that man

bouncing on his toes by the entrance / his molecules

percolating / a blood-spore frenzy / someone says

        Please take off your shoes before entering

white sneakers seeped / in upchuck / eyes ocean waves

divining / left / right / his thin mouth mumble counts

while a diluted song / no one else can hear / sings to him

in the distance / haunting the air like a slow mist / someone

hands him a napkin / to wipe the sweat / another pulls out

a chair / for him to rest / offers cool water / *Welcome brother*

he double tucks his peeling lips in a sneer / and takes it / gulps

        his rage into the black revit / that flexed his pulping

he who thinks himself reaper at the pyre / as citizen of what fuels a threshing marsh rabbit / fear / a dark bouquet of feet

fruiting with lahab and thorns / please report any smoke

suspicious smells / please restrain your curiosity

please do not crawl close / to his hidden hand

And That Fast, You're Thinking about Their Bodies

At a rooftop party, you dance near every edge. Someone drops a ring in glass, in your head the clink of a used bullet, still hot, and that fast the rooftop is covered with wires, riflemen, and you're thinking about mutiny, Mk47s, two cities clawing at each other's bruised throats while boys try to hold your hips, keep dancing. The war is on your hips. Your hands. You wear it all over. You wrap your hair in it. Pluck it from your eyebrows. The rooftop is wide and caring, too rained or sometimes incensed, and you never once think to be afraid of what could arrow a cloud and kill it. You eat volcano rolls, pink pepper goat cheese, and the war enters you. You stare at *Still Life with Flowers and Fruit* and the glade of roses scream war. Here with a doctor and your pregnant aunt who hasn't yet learned English, only speaks in war. Friends in Greensboro get picked up by bored police, get beat up for no reason, and those fists carry war. Job interviews, you carve yourself into a white-known shape and that renaming is a kind of war. You take a passport photo, told to smile without teeth, the flash a bright war. You're on the other side of mercy with your meadows and fluffed spillage, where nights are creamed with saviors. Here everyone rests on roofs graduated and sung, gazing at a sky that won't bleed them. At the beach, you're buried to the neck, practicing dead, snug in your chosen tomb, gulls flittering on all sides, waves fleshing closer, and that fast, you're thinking of a grubby desert girl who placed small stones in her scarf, shook it back and forth, said, *This is what the sea must sound like.*

مالي صمت عن الرثاء

Why I Am Silent about the Lament

by Abdullah Al-Baradouni

They tell me my silence is about lamentation.
I tell them the howling is ugly.

يقولون لي مالي صمتَّ عن الرّثاء
فقلت لهم إنّ العويل قبيحُ

Poetry is only for life and I
felt like singing, not howling.

وما الشعر الاّ للحياة وإنّني
شعرتُ أغنى ما شعرت أنوحُ

How do I call the dead now that between us are hushed
dirt and grave? I am surrounded by mute soil and a mausoleum.

وكيف أنادي ميّتاً حال بينه
وبيني ترابٌ صامتٌ وضريحُ

Howling is only for widows and I am not
like a widow who wails on the silent casket.

وما النّوحُ إلّا للثَكالى ولم أكن
كثكلى على صمت النّعوش تصيحُ

84

Catasterism

Many a night I saw the Pleiads, rising thro' the mellow shade,
Glitter like a swarm of fire-flies tangled in a silver braid.
—LORD TENNYSON

                              Winter is my nightlong field. Cruel, yet,
                    yet after leaving my mother's warm water, I wept
                              snow. And when my tongue tastes
          the first flake, I quiet. Sometimes, I pull from my pocket
               a telescope. In the sky, light
                         collapses, the moon cranked up
          like a cry signal. Last January,
     beneath a sky of scorpions, fish, the bull all scintillating—
I found a girl's body.
          Seven bodies. Sister bodies. Grieving
for the fate of their father, Atlas,
          forced to carry the heavens forever, they kill themselves.
                                        Zeus pins them
                    as a clot
                              of winter stars.
          On the third day, my mother's fat tongue flexes
                    as she sounds the ink blue
                         glyphs of my name, each letter
                    rattling her knucklebones
          as she writes it. A fearful undertaking, Godlike task.
Yet the stars were named
          by people like us. Choose
one word. Say it over
          and over until a blaze builds
in the basin of your mouth:

لنَظم *Alnilam, String of Pearls*
                    راقصة *Ar-Raqis, The Trotting Camel*
                              اخرج من النهر *Achemar, End of the River*

                    I could have been called
               after seven anythings:
                    seven seas, seven heavens,

85

seven ahruf the Holy Qur'an was revealed in. Instead
                    I am named after seven hot orbs
                            of gas, the ghosts
                    of goddesses, daughters dangling
        in sorrow. When I sleep, God threads me through a catasterism.
I am embraced
        as their eighth sister
burning brightly
        in the backdrop of blackness. We evade المنطقة Mintaqa—
                            Orion's pursuit
                        for our love,
                                flash paths for the lost,
        catch and groom the wish a little girl whispers.
                    I wish
                    we could bless ourselves
                into fast comets, firecrackers,
        the pearled wilderness of the moon. And our fathers
tie us in a knotted braid:
        both work too hard,
carry so much weight
        on their shoulders.

                                Fifty years ago, my father learned
                        resistance is found above, in the stars
                            held together by their own gravity.
        How their heat owns the whole night, yet a boy
                can't even keep his home.
                    Since our last move
                he told me, *Each of my wounds
        carries a wounded man*, and—snow in my eyes,
snow in my mouth, wet
        hands iced speech, snow
soaking my socks red—
        I believed him. I want to ask him about the scar.
                        And when do you feel
                    most weary?
                        Do you find yourself

holding up ceilings, sweeping crumpled
                    lifespans off the floor
                         the way I do?
                    Lorca gives me
          a vague trembling of stars, says, *Place these*
in your father's heart.
          Says, *The rose is as white*
as his pain.

                              I see my father's rush: time hugs him
                         tight as he stuffs a suitcase
                              before fajr, sneaks into a smoky slipstream
          from tanks at the corner, stiff-thin shoulders shrouded
                    in morning mist.
                    When he first
          met snow
          his words became corpses. There was no name
for it. In the blizzard,
          his eyes never shut,
face pressed
          into the ground, cold avalanche up his nostrils
                              so he can smell
                    its history.
                         Before he wakes
          I leave a bowl of melted snow by his bed.
                    The winter water
                         coils him into his own
                    constellation.
          From my window, his soul dives into darkness,
scissor kicking
          into a pool of space.
For once, he is held:
          erected mosque, mountained, inexhaustible.
                              In the sky, he isn't a body anymore—
                    endless and ethereal,
                         waiting to be noticed, waiting to be named.

When White Boys Ask to See My Hair

My hair is not taking any visitors right now.

My hair was used as a banner on the moon.

My hair is belly dancing on an auntie's tabletop.

My hair fell off the long line on Mt. Everest trying to take a selfie.

My hair is flipping off an ICE raider after he barges into her favorite deli, arresting her neighbors.

My hair is Medusa's second cousin, the strands slithering along your throat. Avert your gaze for your own good.

My hair was captured from the exotic Manu wilderness and caged for a popular circus show.

My hair is ducking beneath a desk, trying to recall the drills, math sheets falling in a white rain.

My hair escaped an arranged marriage to sail the Red Sea with a crew of burly pirates. She is busy battling maritime brigands and trying not to get lost.

My hair is under siege in Yemen, her home recently bombed, her children buried under the rubble. I am not entirely sure if she will make it out alive.

My hair was abducted by aliens. Rumor has it they spun her into a star. That might be her there, winking down at you.

My hair was mauled on a Tanzanian Safari. I found a few leftover curls flossed between a caracal's fangs.

My hair joined a deep-rooted Bedouin tribe. She enjoys feeding nomadic camels from her palm, became the shaykh's third wife, and sings ancient poetry into campfires. She is happy. I don't think she is coming back.

Ode to Bodega Cats

In the window of my grandfather's corner store,
a cat dressed in my hijab. I feed her titans
of war, pluck Muhammad Ali out her chest wound,

sharpen her a legend in the lake at midnight.
Outside, a wave of Yemeniyat beat a man

after he gropes someone's daughter
in the crowded street. They do it all in abayas.
Full-veiled niqabs. Unstoppable ninjas with

a hundred power-ups. And I know each one
had a bodega cat as a sibling. We learned

the ecology of courage, how to weave one
into our biology, the kind with a third-world
gut and claws out for the cops. What's the word

for a bodega cat's disciple? Vroomed exhaust,
indecent daughter, gray impression on the grid,

ruthless? We keep our scars. They throb
when we pass their glowing eyes, invasive
as a second language. If anyone has taught us

to fend for ourselves, it's the cats on Tremont Ave.
The cats here are made from nothing. One day,

nameless limbs, small square of sidewalk, like a fig
fallen too soon. The next, a gang member's mascot,
beast born from an Arab's love and coked-up rats.

A woman in tragedy also grows that fast,
turns from whimpers to wind in seconds

with the right kind of violence, and after,
makes herself a home for the lost who look
for it. Even the drunks that enter can sense

these cats are off-kilter. They take her on anyway,
leave with one less eye and night terrors.

She gobbles the glass bottles they swing, spits
them out as bullets, laps their blood like
a creature of darkness. She conflates the brute

with the hero. She kills her kids with calmness,
knows how these streets latch onto anything

too green. Bodega Cat Sensei doesn't give a single
fuck. What is there to fear when you've already
licked the edge? I want to be that baddie.

That bitch. That witchy intuition wrung tight
as my braids. Won't find me frozen in the woods

with my scarf stuffed in my mouth. Won't find me
as a scraggle-scaled salmon swimming upriver,
flung into a muddy ditch and left to rot. I'll be funnel

of yellow heat who goes running into a field.
All I want is to be an adequate ancestor

to the Yemeni women who come after. Who visit
my grave with bundles of nut meat for their great-
auntie with the immortal hips, that, myth says, broke

high facility fences and let out all the paperless.
Future long-haired girls gliding above all

that had happened before them. Who will salt
their stories with my own living and become
part of it. So after this lunch break, I'll head to work

and whistle back at the guy who shouts, *Nice tits*
because it's true. I do have nice tits. And a nice

peach emoji, and a birth story, a Khaleesi
walking out the fire. Let them find me dressed
only in leaves, bathing with bodega cats

and their panther mothers, breasts wagging
akimbo. I can't forget those women who clapped

back. Who did not wear worry with each black
layer. Did not let things happen as they usually do
then drop like rotted fruit when it was over.

Notes

A Note on the Translations:
Just one percent of Arab and Asian translation into English has been achieved thus far, so when I first read "From Exile to Exile" online and noticed it was the only poem of Abdullah Al-Baradouni's that had been interpreted and made available, I was immediately inspired to translate more.

Al-Baradouni was a Yemeni poet who contributed greatly to the rising of the Arabic poem. Translating his work empowered and fueled my own writing in many ways, especially when I engaged with his syntax and music. Despite being blind, Al-Baradouni could see what people with sight could not and didn't hesitate to express his own views transparently through his work (much of which was not published during his life).

Recognized Language:
The third section of this poem is written after Marwa Helal's "poem to be read from right to left."

Shaytan Sneaks Bites of My Tuna Sandwich:
The last phrase, "so sweet and so cold" is pulled from William Carlos Williams's poem "This Is Just to Say" referencing the infamous plums in the icebox.

The phrase "lifting her skinny fists like antennas to heaven" is nodding to Godspeed You! Black Emperor's second studio album, *Lift Your Skinny Fists Like Antennas to Heaven*. I was listening to a lot of post-rock while editing this book, which was around the same time as my Whitman Award announcement and the COVID-19 epidemic. The movement in this album, along with a few others (such as Explosions in the Sky's *The World Is Not a Cold Dead Place*) helped me get through not only the revision for this book, but the social distancing and months of quarantine and isolation that followed.

The line "I believed in Shaytan before I believed in the Power Rangers" is a nod to Roy G. Guzmán's "Our Lady of Suyapa."

Pig Flesh:
I reference Khalīl Jubrān's *The Prophet* throughout this collection. In turn, I decided to use the author's true name rather than the well-known "Kahlil Gibran" most have come to recognize in English texts. Jubrān Khalīl Jubrān is the complete signature, but upon his arrival to Boston, an English teacher changed his name on the first day of class, westernizing it. They didn't only purposely misspell it, but misinterpreted it completely.

His full name in Arabic would translate to something close to a "comforting intimate friend." In this way, the correct Arabic spelling withholds his and his father's identity, and is utilized in its originality in my book.

Guide to Gardening Your Roots:
This poem is dedicated to the memory of Nawar Al-Awlaki.

Operation Restoring Hope:
The Saudi Arabian–led military coalition has been conducting airstrikes in Yemen since 2015 in what was known as "Operation Decisive Storm." Saudi Arabia came under increasing international pressure to stop the aerial campaign that has killed and displaced thousands and left cities without power or running water. Since then, "Operation Restoring Hope" began with the goal to protect civilians and intensify relief and medical assistance to the Yemeni people.

The line "For what is prayer but the expansion of our hopes into the living ether?" is taken from Khalīl Jubrān's *The Prophet.*

Yemen Rising as Poorest Country in the World:
A 2019 article from the *United Nations Development Programme* notes that Yemen will become the world's poorest country in 2022 if the conflict continues. Another report, *Assessing the Impact of War in Yemen on Achieving the Sustainable Development Goals*, adds that 79 percent of the population will live under the poverty line and 65 percent will be classified as extremely poor. These articles motivated me to write a poem that showcased the beauty and richness of Yemen, especially that of the south's highly reputed splendor and community, rather than simply focusing on the poverty that strikes it now (making it the largest humanitarian crisis in the world). Southern Yemen was once a land with legendary golden age achievement before the civil war for its territories took place. They advocate only for independence (istiqlal), not secession (infisal), and I would love for people to celebrate that history, to remember it.

Coffee Arabica as a Maelstrom of Endless Aftershocks:
The phrase *haqq al qahwa* is Arabic for *the right of coffee* which is a Yemeni expression for a kickback or bribe.

There was an entire port city in Yemen named after mocha in the fifteenth century, famous for being the major marketplace for coffee.

Coffee arabica is the national flower of Yemen.

at the summit, he finds a nest:
This poem was built around and in conversation with Danez Smith's poem "summer, somewhere," which imagines "boys brown / as rye" in a utopia away from the world that has killed them, in a future redemption. I was inspired by Smith's rhythm and extended sequences to outline qat's relationship with 90 percent of men (and younger boys) in Yemen. The tobacco plant is one of the leading causes of hunger in the country that goes unmentioned, often described as "Yemen chewing itself to death."

Home Security After 9/11:
This poem highlights the significant redeployment of law enforcement in the United States, especially in New York City, after the attacks on September 11, 2001. This included increased suspicion, surveillance, registration, detentions and deportation of Arab and Muslim immigrants. The New York City Police Department has engaged in hundreds of thousands of unreasonable search and seizures without warrants or probable cause. Muslim American homes were infiltrated on a false and unconstitutional premise: that the Islamic religion and practice is a basis for law enforcement scrutiny.

The line "'Red Nation' rises / from a radio, Lil Wayne plopping *Tough luck* into my / breakfast bowl" references the Navy SEAL, Rob O'Neill, who listened to The Game's song "Red Nation" right before killing Osama Bin Laden.

My President Asks Me about Redemption:
This found poem draws its container and some of its language from Khalīl Jubrān's *The Prophet* while also mingling and reworking around my own.

Please Take Off Your Shoes Before Entering:
This poem is in response to the consecutive mass shootings that occurred in a terrorist attack at the Al-Noor mosque and Linwood Islamic Centre in Christchurch, New Zealand, during Friday prayers on March 15, 2019. The attack killed fifty-one Muslims, injured forty-nine, and was livestreamed on Facebook.

The title echoes Chen Chen's poem title "Please take off your shoes before entering do not disturb."

Acknowledgments

Shukran to the following journals and editors who created a space for these poems in their earliest public versions:

The Academy of American Poets: "Heritage Emissary"

The Adroit Journal: "Portrait of This Country"

Ambit: "The Snapping Turtle's in Ta'iz Have Beards"

The American Literary Review: "Muslim Girl with White Guys, Ending at the Edge of a Ridge," "Operation Restoring Hope"

The American Poetry Review: "Muslim with Dog"

The Beloit Poetry Journal: "Recognized Language"

COUNTERCLOCK Journal: "The Etymology of Hair," "Home Security After 9/11," "Middle Eastern Music"

decomP: "After Running Away from Another Marriage Proposal"

Diode Poetry: "When White Boys Ask to See My Hair"

Duende: "Feast, Beginning w/ a Kissed Blade"

The Offing: "Why I Am Silent about the Lament," "Yemen Rising as Poorest Country in the World"

Passages North: "Hidden Bombs in My Coochie"

The Pinch: "Please Take Off Your Shoes Before Entering"

Raleigh Review: "Hunger Wraps Himself," "I Thicken the Room w/ Dim Mirrors & an Alter of Aliens, Waiting for a Sign"

The Rumpus: "Dream Interpretation [*Apricot*]," Dream Interpretation [*Fox*]," "Dream Interpretation [*Sea*]"

Soundings East: "Catasterism"

Split Lip Magazine: "I Crack an Egg"

Spork Press: "Hunting Girliness"

wildness: "And That Fast, You're Thinking about Their Bodies"

Shukran to Jeff Shotts, Chantz Erolin, and the Graywolf family for welcoming me into your pack, and for your insight and support. An extra shukran to Kimberly Glyder for the gorgeous and wilding book cover.

Shukran to Jen Benka and the Academy of American Poets, and to the Civitella Ranieri Foundation. Massive shukran to Harryette Mullen for believing in *The Wild Fox of Yemen* and selecting it as the winner of the Walt Whitman Award.

Shukran to the following foundations and people who have invited and inspired me, and for providing time and space to work on these poems: Lance Cleland and his attentive team at Tin House, along with Jesús Valles, Keith Wilson, Dantiel W. Moniz, Antonio López, Allison Albino, Destiny Birdsong, Monterica Neil, and every Tin Homie that was a part of my scholar crew for their laughter and perspectives; Victoria Chang, Ed Skoog, and Samiya Bashir for their brilliance and encouragement at Idyllwild; Lark Omura, Ana Portnoy, Shangyang Fang, J.J. Hernandez, and all the folks I connected with up at Squaw Valley during those waterfall hikes and emotional late-night cabin readings, as well as Brooke and the elves who took care of us in the mountains like one of their own. Shukran to my MFA fam for your staggering kindness and intellect on and off the page, and to my North Carolina State University mentors Dorianne Laux, Joseph Millar, Belle Boggs, Tyree Daye, Leila Chatti, Arielle Hebert, and Eduardo C. Corral for your intentionality and copious support from my early beginnings.

Shukran to Yahya Frederickson for his generous lending of time, patience, and the Al-Baradouni books.

Shukran to the many Muslim friendships and energies in my New York City, Orlando, and Raleigh masjid communities who drove my imagination for the craft. Those ramblers, lore enthusiasts, and the sahaba of friends and family who allowed me to wonder, becoming part of my perceptions and qalbi.

To the iron-willed Yemeni women who came before me, brandishing an unswerving love and a firm insistence down through the generations, alf shukr.

As Mahmoud Darwish would say, *May poetry and God's name have mercy on us!*

JazakomAllah khair. Blessings to all.

Dedication

For the exiled and fractured people of Yemen, and our families and communities all across the globe—to be guided towards an independent south with goodness and peace between us always.

The people in Yemen are fighting multiple outbreaks, a pandemic, a blockade, an epidemic, a war, and a famine all at the same time, and are on the verge of "not existing as a country." My website (www.threawrites.com/yemenaid) has a list of aid responses by charitable foundations to the ongoing crisis, with donation links for Yemen on their respective sites.

You can also share stories about Yemen on social media to raise awareness, and you can verify that an organization is legitimate by searching the Charity Navigator.

THREA ALMONTASER was born and raised in New York. She holds an MFA from North Carolina State University, where she also earned a TESOL certificate. She was the winner of the Unsilenced Grant for Muslim American Women Writers, the Brett Elizabeth Jenkins Poetry Prize, and the Claire Keyes Poetry Award. *The Wild Fox of Yemen* is the winner of the Walt Whitman Award of the Academy of American Poets. She is a Fulbright scholar and currently teaches English to immigrants and refugees in Raleigh. For more, please visit www.threawrites.com.

The text of *The Wild Fox of Yemen* is set in
Adobe Caslon Pro, Lateef, and Geeza Pro.
Book design by Rachel Holscher.
Composition by Bookmobile Design and Digital
Publisher Services, Minneapolis, Minnesota.
Manufactured by Versa Press on acid-free,
30 percent postconsumer wastepaper.